BUILDING AN UNBREAKABLE MARRIAGE

THE CORNERSTONE PUBLISHING

DR. FESTUS ADEYEYE

BUILDING AN UNBREAKABLE MARRIAGE

Copyright © 2022 by **Dr. Festus Adeyeye**

ISBN: 978-1-952098-98-7

ISBN: 978-1-957809-03-8

Published By Cornerstone Publishing
info@thecornerstonepublishers.com
www.thecornerstonepublishers.com

CONTACT INFORMATION

To order bulk copies of this book, please write to:

Dr. Festus Adeyeye
Adeyeye Evangelical Ministries (AEM)
P.O. Box 810, West Hempstead, NY 11552
E-mail: drfestus@alcminitries.com

CONTENTS

Introduction...7

1. The Bedrock Of Marital Happiness........................13

2. Make The Foundation Right.................................23

3. Common Causes Of Marital Breakdown.................39

4. Making Your Marriage Better...............................53

5. Are We Compatible At All?...................................71

6. Fulfilling Your Marital Roles................................85

7. Managing Your Finances.....................................97

8. Communication: The Tonic Of Intimacy.............103

9. Divorce-Proofing Your Marriage........................117

INTRODUCTION

INTRODUCTION

I s it possible to have an unbreakable marriage? That may be the question on your mind; and rightly so, given its current negative reputation of a high rate of abuse, divorce, dissatisfaction, and gross misunderstandings. The essence of this book is to give you the necessary elements to (i) build a strong and secure marriage despite the current negative tides against the marriage institution, or to (ii) make the best out of your already-better marriage.

Whether you are newly married or you have been married for a lengthy period of time, there is a "here" and a "there." Your "here" is where you are right now and your "there" is where you desire to be, in terms of communication, romance, finances, intimacy, etc. Your "there" is also the plan of God for your marital life.

God's mandate for your "there" is the state of ONENESS. That is God's intent for marriage. Matthew 19:6. Majority of the problems in marriages are as a result of failure to cleave; failure to become one.

The purpose of this book is not to deny the existence of marital challenges; neither does it oversimplify marital issues; rather, it will provide you with simple but effective tools for an enjoyable marriage. My wife and I have been married now for 33 years and counting, with children and grandchildren. At the onset of our marriage, we had our share of marital drama, fights, misunderstandings, and sometimes, seemingly irreconcilable differences. We once sought the help of a Christian marital counselor because we desperately needed help. Our desire to have a better marriage motivated us to learn and do whatever was necessary on our part to make it happen. As time progressed, we began to communicate better, and to understand and love each other, better. Now, we can boldly say that we are enjoying our marriage, and not simply enduring it.

The wisdom principles presented here are time-tested and proven, through years of living by those values. Principles work, and if you apply your heart to pursue those presented throughout this book, they will surely yield positive outcomes for you.

No matter where your marital relationship is right now, it can get better. Are you contemplating a divorce right now? You can still experience a positive change. God specializes in mending broken parts. He specializes in bringing the good out of the ugly and glory out of ashes. You must however be willing and ready to do your part.

It is not a coincidence that the first ministerial accomplishment for Jesus Christ was to provide the best wine in a marriage ceremony. When they ran out of wine, Jesus took what they had and brought about a transformation of water into the best wine ever; a transformation that resulted in joy. The same is true today; if you embrace and allow the wisdom from God's word to guide you actively, you can experience a positive change. Once my wife and I got to the point where we contemplated divorce in the early part of our marriage, we agreed to passionately learn and put into practice, these unbreakable principles that have brought us to the great union that we have today. Our experience of a marriage that was about to break apart then, is now being used to guide and strengthen innumerable marriages, globally.

I know what it is for couples to be trapped in a life of unending arguments and misunderstandings. I know what it is for couples to stay together in the same house, but live as strangers. If that is where you are right now; change is possible. God can take your mess and make a miracle out of it.

ONE

THE BEDROCK OF MARITAL HAPPINESS

ONE

THE BEDROCK OF MARITAL HAPPINESS

"Therefore a man shall leave his father and mother and be joined to his wife, and they shall become one flesh."
(Genesis 2:24)

Building an unbreakable marriage begins with a good comprehension of the meaning and purpose of the marital union. Most of the marital problems that we witness or are privy to, originate from a lack of understanding of these two values. Without this requisite foundation, many things are bound to go wrong and a marital relationship could sooner or later be subject to severe difficulties, or even worse, come to an end.

Many people get married simply because they consider it the necessary thing to do at a particular point in their lives, or because it is expected at a particular stage of their relationship. Sadly, such people have a distorted knowledge of the institution of marriage. Nowadays, many marriages are full of crisis and confusion and are nothing but an abuse of God's original blueprint. For that reason, unraveling the secrets of marital bliss requires the examination of the fundamental truths surrounding the institution of marriage, as told in Scriptures.

WHAT YOU SHOULD KNOW ABOUT MARRIAGE

1. GOD IS THE ORIGINATOR OF MARRIAGE.

Marriage was not man's idea. It did not originate from Adam. In fact, Adam himself seemed to have no clue of his limitations as a single person, until God intervened on his behalf. It was God who said, "It is not good that man should be alone; I will make him a helper comparable to him" (Genesis 2:18). This was a provision God made out of love and concern for man's wellbeing. Therefore, marriage is not a mere cultural or traditional observance; it is a divine institution; it is God's special gift to mankind.

Three very important connotations emerge from this truth about the origin of marriage.

* First, contrary to many erroneous beliefs, God designed marriage to be a beautiful, blessed, and fulfilling experience. He created it to be enjoyable. "Every good gift and every perfect gift is from above…" (James 1:17). God did not design marriage to be a sorrowful and regrettable experience as many have come to see it. The Bible states that "the blessing of the LORD makes one rich, and He adds no sorrow with it" (Proverbs 10:22). Proverbs 18:22 is even more specific in saying, "He who finds a wife finds a good thing, and obtains favor from the LORD. Maybe your marital relationship is everything but good at this moment; but having this understanding will help your resolve for a better outcome. As stated in the introduction, the very first miracle that Christ performed was for a couple, at their wedding ceremony (John 2:1-11). This is to

communicate to us how important marriage is to God; how vested He is in the marital union, and most importantly for us, how much of divine power and visitation we can attract to our lives, by entering into the marriage covenant the God-ordained way.

- Secondly, since the marriage institution originated from God, it is imperative to operate marriage based on God's prescriptions and principles. Marriage is much deeper than two people falling in love and choosing to spend the rest of their lives together. In fact, Paul the Apostle affirmed that there is a great mystery involved in the marital covenant (Ephesians 5:32). It is not just a fusion of hearts, but also, a fusion of lives and destinies towards the accomplishment of a divine agenda. As John Piper explains, "God patterned marriage purposefully after the relationship between His Son and the church, which He planned from eternity."

- The third connotation from the origin of marriage is that it must be entered into with reverential respect for the order of God. It should be entered into with the overriding desire to please God and abide by His guidelines for marital life. While unfeigned love for one's spouse is expected to be the major driver of most actions in marriage, the ultimate motive must be the desire to please God at every point in time. When pleasing God becomes the ultimate goal of both parties involved in a marital relationship it makes the journey easier. A couple will not be moved by any momentary unpleasantness, when they know that God is the overall Master of their relationship.

2. MARRIAGE REQUIRES MATURITY

Many people enter into marriage without having developed the requisite character traits for sustaining a lifelong relationship, or for managing the routine issues and challenges of marriage. In many instances, many want to be married and enjoy the lifestyle of the singles, simultaneously. That is, they do not wish to relinquish their liberty, privacy, carefree living, tantrums, temperamental attitude, lack of accountability, etc. In essence, they want to enjoy the privileges of marriage without sacrificing habits peculiar to the single life. Inevitably, this creates problems in their relationship. Having an unbreakable marriage requires each person in a marital relationship to embrace the responsibilities that come with marriage.

The developmental level of the two people entering into a marital union is very important. In the first marriage instituted by God, Adam was a full-grown man who was gainfully employed, capable of taking care of himself, and able to appreciate the wife to be given to him. Similarly, God brought a woman to Adam, not a girl to be nursed to adulthood. Part of the distortion of marriage today is the union of "boys" and "girls." Although some level of physical maturity is required, in this instance, "boys and girls" is a reference to spiritual and emotional maturity and not age.

3. MARRIAGE PARTNERS ARE BOUND TO SHARE SIMILARITIES AND DIFFERENCES.

Majority of the issues that couples often have in marriage have to do with their differences in personalities. Men sometimes wonder why their wives do not think, act and process things like them and vice versa. God did not create the first marriage partners in the same way. Even though a part of Adam was used to form Eve thus establishing a link between the two, the patterns He adopted to create them were different. The differences in the male and female genders, particularly in behavioral patterns, were deliberately programmed by God to achieve His goal for marriage. If He wanted the man and the woman to think and act the same way, he would not have created them in different ways.

While we have a detailed description of how man was made, not much is revealed about the creation of the woman, other than the fact that a rib was taken from the man. By inference therefore, if it has pleased God to make the man and the woman different, that must be the best way for His purpose for them to be accomplished. Wisdom therefore demands that marital partners understand, appreciate, and seek ways to maximize their differences, rather than complain about them.

Differences notwithstanding, we know that both the man and the woman also share some physical similarities (which can be interpreted as shared interests), and more importantly, spiritual similarities. Both the man and the woman are perfect products of God.

4. BOTH PARTNERS IN MARRIAGE ARE MEANT TO COMPLEMENT AND COMPLETE EACH OTHER.

God gave prominence to selfless service in the vision of the marriage institution. It was the necessity of a fitting helper that brought about marriage. Simply put, God brings partners together for each to help the other to fulfill God's purpose for their lives, and to be their best selves.

Marriage is therefore a union of two imperfect people coming together for a lifetime of covenant commitment. God saw that Adam had a need and it was in meeting that need that Eve was created. Clearly, Adam could never be complete without the part that was taken from him. Similarly, Eve was not created independently; the mold from which her frame was cast was taken from the man, making her his helper, and not his superior. Both are part of each other and that is why the Scripture says that no man hates his own flesh (Ephesians 5:29).

Consequently, when God brings two people together, His primary goal is to ensure that they both complement and complete each other.

5. MARITAL PARTNERS MUST LEAVE TO CLEAVE.

Most times, when we hear of leaving to cleave, all that comes to our mind is disengagement from parental control, parental influence, and of course, place of abode. This is absolutely true, even though many people still prefer having it both ways. They still want to be "mummy's boy" and "daddy's girl" and at the same time be married and starting their own family. Marriage is not however divorcing your parents or other family members. It is learning to prioritize your marital relationships above them.

The marriage relationship is a different level of relationship from others. It exists completely on a different realm of living. Accordingly, it is expected that the focus of either spouse should exclusively be how they will forge a unique home life, culture, and destiny, for themselves.

Wisdom demands that they must both detach from previous family ties and close relationships with members of the opposite gender. There is also the need to disconnect from some psychological "hangovers." Examples are extreme attachment to family traditions and practices, and comparisons with previous relationships.

There are individuals who expect their marriage to be an automatic extension of the lifestyle, atmosphere, and practices that they grew up with in their parents' home. They are so tied to past traditions that they may want to impose same on their spouses. Others with previous relationships, such as former widows/widowers, may hold on tightly to memories - memories that they continue to use as a gauge for their current marriage. This will eventually lead to an unhealthy marriage.

6. BOTH THE MAN AND THE WOMAN ARE MEANT TO BECOME ONE FLESH.

"This people I have formed for Myself; They shall declare My praise" (Isaiah 43:21). The ultimate goal of God in bringing two people with uniquely different attributes together in marriage, is for them to bring glory to His name through their union. However, this cannot happen until the couple consciously and selflessly work towards harmonizing their differences, aspirations, and potentials. Once that has happened, they can purposefully move forward in a common direction, for the fulfillment of their destinies.

All of the points described above are included in God's blueprint for marriage. Collectively, those attributes make it easier for couples to understand the true meaning of marriage and to establish a proper foundation for marital happiness. Delving into the points also enables couples to identify the root causes of most of the problems that beset their marital union.

TWO
MAKE THE FOUNDATION RIGHT

TWO

MAKE THE FOUNDATION RIGHT

"But did He not make them one, Having a remnant of the Spirit? And why one?
He seeks godly offspring. Therefore take heed to your spirit, And let none deal treacherously with the wife of his youth."
(Malachi 2:15)

Foundation is very crucial to any adventure in life. When the foundation is right, the likelihood of succeeding is very high. In building a house, one of the primary concerns that you need to pay careful attention to is the foundation. A house is only as strong as the foundation upon which it is built. This is also true in a marriage. The success of the marriage is largely dependent on the foundation of the union. This speaks especially of the reasons for getting married

People marry for several reasons. To some, it is merely a social contract to be run and guided by traditional beliefs. For some, it is simply an avenue for child-bearing. And to others, especially in the Western world, it is comparable to a business — you stay in it as long as everything is working in your favor, or as long as you find it interesting; and once you encounter problems or become bored, you find a way to opt out.

WRONG REASONS FOR GETTING MARRIED

Marriage is certainly a sweet experience; but it depends on the "cutlery" with which you eat it. There are times when people enter into marriage for the wrong reasons and deviate from the tenets of the marital union. By so doing, they lay faulty marital foundations, and consequently, they experience marital crises.

Why do you want to get married? Your reason(s) should not be any of the flawed motives listed below. And if you are already married, be encouraged to revisit and realign your motives with God's ultimate purpose for marriage.

Some erroneous reasons for which people get married include:

1. TO FULFIL THEIR PARENTS' EXPECTATIONS OR TO ESCAPE PARENTAL CONTROL.

It is true that there are parents who, even in this age and time, still mount undue pressure on their children to get married by all means. In some cases, the children themselves know that they are not ready or, it could be that God has not led them to anyone yet. Sadly, some of such children sometimes give in to pressure and marry out of desperation. There are also parents who arrange spouses for their children without following an adequate process of godly selection. Others marry so that their parents can accept that they are truly grown and should no longer be controlled.

2. TO HAVE CHILDREN IN A MORE ACCEPTABLE WAY.

This has to do with people who passionately desire to have children, but do not want to do so out of wedlock. That means that they marry mainly for procreation and do not bother themselves with the requirements for a successful marriage. Of course, having children out of wedlock is unbiblical; however, you must not rush into marriage for that singular purpose only.

3. TO PROVIDE A FATHER OR MOTHER FOR EXISTING CHILDREN.

There are single parents who have bought into the lie that their children cannot have a balanced upbringing without having mother and father figures. While it is ideal that both parents are available to raise a child, it is not a justification for being desperate to marry. Some women in particular, have been made to believe that their sons will never be good men, unless there is a male influence in their lives. Yet, God has promised to be a father to the fatherless.

Furthermore, there have been cases of successful men and women who were raised by single parents, as well as those of wayward children who were raised by both parents. I am not advocating for single parenthood though; my point is that desiring a mother or father figure for your children is not enough reason to get married. Marriage is much more than that!

4. TO GET BACK AT THEIR EX-SPOUSE.

This relates to those who marry hastily on the rebound. Marriage is too sacred and too significant to be entered into, to spite another. Sooner or later, the vengeful spouse might cause more self-harm than good.

5. TO CHANGE THEIR STATUS QUO FOR SOCIETAL ACCEPTANCE.

In many societies around the world, it is common for married people to be accorded special recognition and privileges. Therefore, it is not surprising that this is what drives some people into marriage - the desire to change their status or to give the appearance of stability and responsibility.

6. TO HAVE SEX ON DEMAND.

This may seem funny, but it happens. It should be noted, however, that while sex has been said to be a vital part of the marital package, there is no guarantee that it will always be available. A number of factors contribute to this. And even when sex is accessible, it is not as simple as flipping a light switch; it is usually a combination of romance, intimacy and other essential in-betweens.

7. TO HAVE A COMFORTABLE LIFE.

Some people believe that having a wife or a husband is a quick way to better their finances, via the sharing of bill payments and other expenses. Firstly, you are supposed to develop and invest in yourself to be self-sufficient before marriage. Marriage does not make up for your lack of competence; it amplifies it. Of course, your spouse can be a support to you financially and otherwise; but it should not be the reason for getting married. You should not enter into marriage broke, expecting to be fixed by your spouse. Instead, you should endeavor to add value to your spouse.

THERE IS STILL HOPE

Please note that the motives above are not to disparage anyone. If you married because of any of those reasons, as long as you made a vow before God and man, there is still hope for your marriage. Your life and marriage can still have joy!

Having the understanding of the purpose for marriage will help to reshape your thinking and revamp your relationship. The reasons for which God instituted marriage can be summarized into the seven motives itemized below. They are all vital to repairing the foundation of your marriage. They may be viewed as the blessings of marital life. You may consider them to be the roles that God expects each partner to play in a marriage (we will elaborate on roles in a later chapter). Finally, you may view it as an outline of what to expect in a marital union.

The last three perspectives are particularly important because marriage is an all-inclusive package of blessings, responsibilities, and expectations. However, what sometimes causes problems in a marriage is an individual's supposition that he/she can decide to cherry-pick only aspects of the marital package that suits them. This, more often than not, leaves their spouse disappointed and frustrated.

WHY DID GOD INSTITUTE MARRIAGE?

1. PARTNERSHIP

This is the primary purpose of the marital union. God, who created man, clearly declared that "it is not good that man should be alone" (Genesis 2:18). R.C Sproul notes that this is the first negative judgment we find in the Bible - the judgment against loneliness. By implication, man is only in the best state he can be, when he has a lifelong companion and helpmate with him. The marriage union was therefore established to actualize this.

Marriage is a binding commitment by a man and a woman, to remain in covenant companionship with each other for the rest of their lives. God designed it to be the best and highest form of friendship on earth, through its constancy and possibilities.

In marriage, each partner lives to seek the other's interests. They see each other, not as superior and subordinate, but as "…heirs together of the grace of life…" (1 Peter 3:7). They freely share their lives, dreams, hopes, aspirations, concerns, joys, pains, and expectations with each other – with the restful assurance that each will forever do the other good, not harm.

Couples in partnership talk and listen to each other, laugh, work, play, and pray together, blessing each other. They counsel, support, correct, inspire, and edify each other. They also encourage each other to be the best they can be.

True marriage partners generally root for each other, look out for each other, thirst for each other and rest in each other's love, knowing full well that they are each other's number one and everlasting fan. They care for each other in sickness and in health and through the good and the trying times. This is why Ecclesiastes 4:9-11 says, "Two are better than one, because they have a good reward for their labor. For if they fall, one will lift up his companion.

But woe to him who is alone when he falls, For he has no one to help him up. Again, if two lie down together, they will keep warm; But how can one be warm alone?"

Unfortunately some people prefer to stay aloof physically or emotionally, despite being married. They find it hard to share their space, time and feelings with their spouse, nor do they take adequate time to know what is going on in their spouse's world. This obviously defeats the purpose of marriage and inevitably breeds crisis.

Moreover, the fact that marriage is a partnership and not a servant-slave relationship means that there certainly will be moments of divergent perspectives, opinions and ideas. This is perfectly normal and healthy. In fact, it has been rightly said that if two partners always agree, it means that one of them is unnecessary.

2. PROTECTION

Marital partners are brought together to form a wall of defense around each other. This defense is to help ward off physical, spiritual, emotional and psychological attacks. Enemies, whether spiritual or physical, are known to find solitary people as soft targets or easy preys; but when they know that an individual has company, they think twice before they attack.

The first and most important form of defense that marriage is expected to provide is protection against sin - sexual sin, in particular. Paul the Apostle wrote, "Now concerning the things whereof ye wrote unto me: It is good for a man not to touch a woman. Nevertheless, to avoid fornication, let every man have his own wife, and let every woman have her own husband... Defraud ye not one the other, except it be with consent for a time, that ye may give yourselves to fasting and prayer; and come together again, that Satan tempt you not for your incontinency" (1 Corinthians 7:1-2, 5) (KJV).

Aside from protection from sexual sins, marriage also helps to guard against the wiles and snares of the wicked one, as marriage partners pray for each other and help to watch over each other's soul, so that neither is led astray. Many today would have had their life and ministry extinguished by the fiery darts of the enemy, if not for the timely prayer, observation and admonition of their spouses. Everyone has had moments of weakness which the devil could have swiftly capitalized on, but for the timely intervention of their spouses.

Marriage also helps to safeguard our psychological balance when the whole world seems to be against us. The unflinching love, support, and encouragement we receive from our life companion helps to stabilize our minds and keep us from depression or low self-esteem.

3. PROCREATION

It is God's desire for us to be fruitful, multiply, replenish the earth, and have unhindered dominion. Procreation is an essential aspect of marriage because it helps to swell the Kingdom workforce for fulfilling God's agendas on earth. Like begets like. Hence, children of God are not expected to give birth just for the sake of it; we give birth to populate the earth with "holy seeds." Malachi 2:15 (KJV) clearly emphasizes this: "And did not he make one? Yet had he the residue of the spirit. And wherefore one?

That he might seek a godly seed..."

This expectation of godly seeds explains one of the reasons God has a special interest in marriage. John Piper explains, "God's purpose in making marriage the place to have children was never merely to fill the earth with people, but to fill the earth with worshippers of the true God... When the focus of marriage becomes "Make children disciples of Jesus," the meaning of marriage in relation to children is not mainly "Make them," but "Make them disciples." And the latter can happen even where the former does not."

It becomes so easy then, to understand why the Bible describes children as the heritage of God. And it is indeed a great privilege that every couple can partner with God in forming, birthing, raising and protecting this heritage.

However, although this is one of the reasons for establishing the marital covenant, the lack of it should not be the determining factor of happiness in the marriage. Husbands and wives should be determined to enjoy their union, with or without children. If you are having difficulty in this area right now, I pray for divine intervention for a speedy answer.

4. PLEASURE

This is one area that must be emphasized, especially for people of faith. The subject of pleasure in marriage has been a major cause of concern, scandal, crisis, and even breakup. There are so many people who get married and do not understand that sexual intimacy is an intrinsic component of the marital package. They want marriage but see sex as a dirty and shameful act, reserved only for the carnally minded. They believe that sex should only be for procreation and nothing else.

Yet, nowhere in the Bible is there a condemnation of sex within marriage. Sex is actually one of the special gifts of God to every married couple. They are the only ones allowed to enjoy this powerful, thrilling and bonding activity without shame or guilt. Sex that is condemned is such that is before or outside of marriage.

Moreover, the Bible does not say sex for the married should only be for procreation. Rather, it encourages them to have it as much as possible. For instance, Proverbs 5:15-19 says, "Drink waters out of thine own cistern, and running waters out of thine own well. Let thy fountains be dispersed abroad, and rivers of waters in the streets. Let them be only thine own, and not strangers' with thee. Let thy fountain be blessed: and rejoice with the wife of thy youth. Let her be as the loving hind and pleasant roe; let her breasts satisfy thee at all times; and be thou ravished always with her love."

Did you observe how many times the husband is encouraged to be satisfied with the wife's breasts? It says at all times or always. As mentioned earlier, even Paul the Apostle who had the special grace to be a eunuch, advises married couples on how frequently they must make love, saying; "Let the husband render unto the wife due benevolence: and likewise also the wife unto the husband. The wife hath not power of her own body, but the husband: and likewise also the husband hath not power of his own body, but the wife. Defraud ye not one the other, except it be with consent for a time, that ye may give yourselves to fasting and prayer; and come together again, that Satan tempt you not for your incontinency" (1 Corinthians 7:3-5).

The message from the above is clear. Sex among married couples should only be withheld for a brief moment of jointly agreed spiritual exercise. Otherwise, it should be enjoyed as much as possible, because each member of the marriage union has complete rights over the other's body. Avoid jumping into spiritual activity that will deny your spouse sex without first discussing and agreeing together. I am not surprised that the scriptures encourage married couples to enjoy each other's love unceasingly. God has filled our bodies with powerful hormones and nerve endings that not only drive sexual cravings, but also fill us with immense pleasure; pleasure that comes with lots of physical, psychological, and emotional benefits.

Once again, pleasure is an integral part of marriage. When you do not allow your spouse to get enough of it, that is actually a sin. You cannot remove, reduce or ration the marital package, without frustrating your spouse.

5. Perfection

Marriage has been said to be a union of two imperfect people. The beauty, however, is that God ensures that the two perfectly complement and complete each other with their unique abilities, mentalities and proclivities. Jay Adams, in explaining this, said, "Together they form one complete unit. As they come together physically, intellectually, emotionally, there is a wholeness that did not exist before. They are fused into one." Each partner in a true, God-ordained marriage is an extension and completer of the other. That is why couples should not see their differences as a problem but rather as a blessing. Where one lacks, the other complements and completes.

The point here is that men and women are formed and wired differently such that what each lacks the other can supply in abundance. Bearing this in mind, people must stop disparaging their spouses for being different or trying to make their spouse like themselves. At the onset of our marital relationship, I fought my wife for her unique differences and tried to make her conform to my own way. Not until I learned this principle of harnessing her uniqueness as a needed blessing to my life. God made them male and female, not just in appearance but in thinking and inclinations – and that is exactly how best His purpose for them can be accomplished. Husbands and wives cannot and must not be exactly like each other. As the Bible says, "If the whole body were an eye, where were the hearing? If the whole were hearing, where were the smelling? (1 Corinthians 12:17) (KJV).

6. PROSPERITY

One of the reasons two are said to be better than one is because they have a good reward for their labor. They can think together, plan together and work together towards living a life of abundance and great accomplishments. You are of course required to discover and derive your purpose and completeness from your relationship with Christ. You are required to be matured and invest in yourself to be financially, mentally, emotionally and spiritually matured even before marriage. However, your output will increase

when the two of you come together. Testimonies abound
of those who by the innovativeness, judiciousness and
meticulousness of their spouses have not only seen their
riches better managed, but also multiplied.

It is particularly gladdening that the Scripture says that
"He who finds a wife finds a good thing, And obtains
favor from the Lord" (Proverbs 18:22). This means that
there is a special endowment upon a man, once he finds
the right person. Once you are able to connect with a
woman that is meant for you as a man, automatic favor
to excel comes upon you. The same goes for a woman.
When Abram's name was changed to Abraham, God did
not stop there; He also ensured that Sarai's name was
changed to Sarah.

7. POWER

Marriage is an avenue to attract unlimited supernatural
power from God to accomplish greater exploits on earth.
Ecclesiastes 4:12 says, "Though one may be overpowered
by another, two can withstand him…" This means that
marriage positions a couple to record such victories and
breakthroughs that they might not have been able to record
as single individuals. Indeed, there have been testimonies
of spouses who obtained solutions to longstanding
problems through the support of each other in prayer.

With a couple's united purpose, prayer, daily communion
with God, and commitment to His work, there will be
a continuous overflow of God's power for victory,
dominion, and miracles, in their household. Jesus Christ
in Matthew 18:19 assures, "Again I say to you that if two

of you agree on earth concerning anything that they ask, it will be done for them by My Father in heaven."

This speaks about the power of agreement and unity in general. However, if there could be so much power in the prayer of those who are in momentary agreement and who may even have little acquaintance with each other, how much more will it be for those in a permanent covenant relationship of marriage?

THREE

COMMON CAUSES OF
MARITAL BREAKDOWN

THREE

COMMON CAUSES OF MARITAL BREAKDOWN

Although marriage can be a delightful and sweet experience, it is also subject to several challenges that can tear it apart, if care is not taken. Like any other relationship, marriage must be handled wisely and given proper attention to avoid a breakdown. Sometimes couples unintentionally grow apart for lack of proper attention and care. No matter how long a couple has been married, the relationship still requires intentional daily care and attention to avoid breakdown. There are several factors responsible for marital breakdown.

1. COUPLES ENTERING MARRIAGE ARE EQUIPPED ONLY WITH THE WORLD'S UNBIBLICAL MARITAL PATTERN.

This is when we enter the marriage relationship with this world's unbiblical philosophies, mindsets, and value systems. Among such are:

The world's pattern of 50/50 performance. This mindset requires each person in the marriage to contribute 50/50 in all things. That is why I do not believe in referring to one's spouse as "the better half." Your spouse is not your better half but your 100 percent partner. The 50/50 world pattern is a system where acceptance is based upon performance. Roles are to be shared equally among husband and wife. Bills are supposed to be shared equally between husband and wife. It then becomes a union of "you do your part, and I will do mine." Each person's worth in the relationship is validated when you live up to your assigned contributions.

Respect for each other is based on how well you perform the expected assigned duties. In God's Kingdom, marriage and acceptance are to be based solely on the marital covenant and agape love, based on the principle of oneness. God expects 100/100 and not 50/50. God expects and demands both parties to be responsible by committing fully to the home with hearts knitted together in covenant commitment. Kingdom marital relationship is not based on things and performance but total commitment to the vision and goals of the union.

When you are fully committed to your spouse and the marriage, you will not be forced to give what is required for the union's success. The lack of or the supply of financial contributions do not validate anyone's position in the home. In the unbiblical mindset of the world, affection is given when one feels it is deserved or earned. Or when one is perceived as a provider. At the same time, God wants us to love each other and respect each other unconditionally.

We got involved in settling a matter for a couple, and the wife accused the husband of not being man enough. Her definition of not "man enough" was that his earning power was insufficient. Even though the man works very hard to maintain the family, his best is considered inadequate. Because of that, she judged his manhood and husbandhood based on his financial contribution.

The pattern of 50/50 is unbiblical and self-destruct because of:

- Inability to meet unreal expectations. A spouse may be confronted with real-life challenges that will affect their ability to perform to such unrealistic expectations in the real world. There could be a job loss, a disability that prevents a spouse from fulfilling certain obligations, etc. The inability to perform to expectations can cause disappointment in your spouse, paralyzing your performance. She or he may conclude that "if she or he is not doing anything, neither will I."

- Demanding that your spouse meet you halfway can reduce marriage to a business-like arrangement, instead of a union based on covenant love.

- This mindset can create the tendency of focusing on the weakness in one's spouse, thereby causing it to stand as an obstacle to authentic agape love.

2. Refusal to drop the baggage of the past.

In conflict resolution for couples, a common mistake we have noticed is allowing the past to torment their present relationship. For example, someone in an abusive relationship in the past, either with a fiancée or an ex-husband/wife, can interpret the actions of the new spouse through the lens of the behaviors of their past fiancée or ex-spouse. This is what I call seeing your new husband

41

"John" with the lens of your previous husband "Jack." It would help if you were healed from the emotional hurt of the past relationships and their effect on your emotional reactions before embarking on a marital journey with someone else. There was a case of a woman who would always tell the husband during a simple normal argument: "Do you want to hit me? If I see you lift your hand and touch me, it will be your last. I can see you are about to hit me in the face, right?" She later confessed to the fact that she usually had a flashback on how the ex-husband physically abused her.

This can also happen to a man. You need to intentionally open up about the emotional hurt and abusive patterns from your past relationships. Seek the help of the Holy Spirit in prayers for healing and talk about it with a marriage counselor if it has become a serious problem. Give your new spouse a chance to prove herself and never compare them or judge them as your previous spouse.

Another example of how the past can tear relationships apart, is the inability to divorce yourself from the bad advice from your parents, family, and friends and the bad image of marriage seen during your upbringing. For example, the final discussion on the night of her wedding between a lady and her mother went like this. 'My daughter, men are never to be trusted, so never open up all of your heart to any man. Make sure to always have what is called your own in the marriage. Keep your own money and have your secrets, etc." The mother had a bad experience in her marital relationship and concluded that all men were like her husband. Psalms 116:11 says, "…I said in my haste; all men are liars." Is it true that all men are liars? We have several liars, but that all men are liars is a hasty conclusion. We have several abusive men, but all men are not abusive.

Whenever you start a marriage with a flawed and abused mind, the marriage is already doomed to break apart because of a faulty foundation. No matter how close someone is to you or how nice they are, never take their failed experience as your philosophy of life. David refused to wear Saul's armor to fight his own battle. He used what he had tested instead. If the armor did not work for Saul, why would it work for David? The strategies that did not work for someone probably will not work for you. Enter into your marital union with the scriptural mindset that the two shall no longer be two, but one. If you discover unusual behavior from your spouse, then deal with it truthfully and prayerfully as prescribed in the word of God. You should both develop and create your own marital experience with the help of the Holy Spirit.

3. FAILURE TO PROPERLY NAVIGATE THROUGH INEVITABLE DIFFICULTIES AND TRIALS.

It is no secret that marriages face everyday challenges and difficulties. Even if you were married in heaven, you would still face some problems. These challenges can be economical, career-related, or related to raising children. Misunderstandings can happen in any marriage. Failure to prepare and the inability to respond appropriately, may inevitably lead to the end of the marriage. There are two failures in our response to trial, challenges, and misunderstandings:

There is the failure to anticipate the reality of difficulties and problems. There is the failure to respond properly to difficulties and concerns. Your response to difficulties and challenges will either drive you apart or bind you together.

While couples must maintain an attitude of love and godly expectations and avoid being negative in their attitude and expectations, they should also know that difficulties and challenges are real in any relationship. They should know that there will be times of highs and times of lows. It is not atypical or unique to them if they experience occasional life struggles or tend to argue or fight. They should expect that offenses and challenges will come. No matter the conflicts, it can strengthen the union, instead of tearing it apart, if appropriately handled. Couples should be proactively prepared for conflicts and properly communicate, to navigate their challenges.

This mindset will guide the couple to live wisely, watch, and be alert. Some couples respond to a problem by suppressing, denying, or postponing dealing with it. That will amount to postponing the battles that should be dealt with in the present into the future. It will resurface in the future with a greater damaging effect on the relationship. Anticipate that challenges will come. Proactively map out strategies for conflict resolution whenever they arise. And never respond to the problem by blaming or attacking each other. To avoid creating more problems when confronted with a problem, you must have a plan to move through those periods without rejecting or withdrawing from your spouse.

4. Extramarital affairs.

Although extramarital affairs include having sexual affairs known as adultery, it is more than adultery. The root foundation of extramarital affairs is simply a search for fulfillment outside of the marriage or an escape from the reality of your marriage into a non-existing one. It is anything or anyone that entices you for satisfaction outside of your marital covenant. So, extramarital affairs take many different forms.

- Activities affair. Any activity that takes your focus, time, energy, and resources away from your marital responsibilities, and tends to give you relief from the daily grind of your home.

- Materialism affair. This is excessive attachment to material things that shift your focus from the essentiality of your marital covenant commitments.

- Career affair. This is when a spouse gives undue attention to their job/career at the expense of the marriage. As important as having a good career/job is for your family's financial stability, money cannot replace love. While your family needs your financial support, they also need your physical presence and the emotional stability it provides. It is advisable to balance your work with your family life. Do not be married to your career/job while neglecting the upbringing of your children and emotional closeness with your spouse. Money can provide lots of support and goodies in a relationship, but money cannot provide joy, happiness, and the emotional stability of having you.

- Family affair. This is when a spouse is unduly attached to the extended family more than their spouse. Some people make their marital home an extension of the home where they were raised. Their parents and siblings control their marital home, causing the spouse to compete for attention with the siblings or parents. While no one is expected to divorce his or her parents, siblings, and some good friends, never give them undue influence and control over your spouse. No matter how godly or nice, parents will always be biased in supporting their children in the relationship. The creator of marriage understands this when He says, "the man should leave his mother and father and be joined to his wife" and vice versa.

- Love affairs (adultery). This is when a spouse is involved in a love affair with someone else outside of the marriage. It is known as adultery or infidelity. This is very damaging and sinful. It is very dangerous to you, your spouse, and your children. If you are in such a problem, repent of it, turn your heart to God, and seek help where necessary. Guard against getting into any romantic, affectionate friendship with anyone other than your spouse. It causes soul ties, destroys commitment, wastes resources, and kills trust.

5. SELFISHNESS IN MARRIAGE.

Self-centeredness is a destroyer and a devourer of love. It causes love to fade away and be eroded. Successful relationships are never self-centered. We live in a society that encourages excessive self-worship and self-entitlement. This is the mindset to be overly committed to ourselves. Just "me, myself, and I." The new triune. Every marital problem is a spin-off of this one problem. Jesus called it a hardness of your heart in Matthew 19:8. For instance, illicit affairs result from someone who is only concerned about meeting their sexual urge. Mishandling of finances, neglect, abuse, etc., all stem from self-centeredness; which when we justify it, further complicates matters.

"If people know the depth of my pain, they will be more caring." "Nobody can possibly understand what I have been through." "It is because of my personality type." "It is a mid-life crisis." The bottom line is wanting what you want when you want it. When you get to this point, you become unreasonable and accepting of your behavior. Although you will not accept it in others, you will justify and excuse yourself for them. This is corrosive and will ultimately lead to a breakdown in your relationship. A successful marriage requires you to look out for your spouse's good, even above yours.

"Let each of you look not only to his own interests but also to the interests of others."

Wake up daily to look for how to support your spouse in all things. When you do so and your spouse does so, the equation of mutual reciprocity will be balanced. Submit the lordship of your heart to God by dying daily to the flesh.

Self-centeredness dies through the growing knowledge of God. As you study God's word, let it be a mirror to reflect your true self. And be ready to change where necessary.

Self-centeredness is also dealt with by growing in love and fear of God.

We saw that the wedding at Cana ran out of wine until Jesus stepped in for a turnaround. Wine is a type of joy. He can do the same for you today. The key for the turnaround can be found in John 2:5. "His mother said to the servants, 'Do whatever he tells you.'" The same is true today. If you would do whatever the word of God says to do concerning marital relationships, you are bound to experience a marital breakthrough instead of a marital breakdown. You are bound to experience joy, no matter what has dried up in your relationship. Make practicing God's word a priority in your relationship.

6. LACK OF TRANSPARENCY AND TRUST.

Transparency is one of the keys to breakthroughs in marriage. Amos 3:3. "Can two walk together except they be agreed?" Agreement in any relationship, including marital, involves transparency. This is when nothing is hidden from each other. Couples should always endeavor to avoid keeping any secrets from each other. Be transparent with your time, financial transactions, and relationships outside. This requires being accountable to each other. The more transparent you are in your marriage, the more trust is built.

7. LACK OF ACCOUNTABILITY.

Proverbs 11:4 (ESV): Where no wise guidance is, the people falleth; But in the multitude of counselors, there is safety. Marriages break down when either party is not accountable to anyone. Firstly, both must be accountable to God; secondly, accountable to each other; and finally have an authority over them to whom they are accountable. As a matter of necessity, every couple should have someone they respect and honor as a mentor in their lives - someone to whom both agree to be accountable. Your spouse should know someone you are accountable to and whom they can approach whenever there is a major disagreement. And it is someone for whom you have a great deal of respect, honor, and willingness to obey. Having a spouse who is not accountable to anyone is sitting in a moving car with no brake. It is dangerous.

Hebrews 13:17 (NLT) says, "Obey your spiritual leaders, and do what they say. Their work is to watch over your souls, and they are accountable to God. Give them a reason to do this with joy and not with sorrow. That would certainly not be for your benefit."

A man or woman who cannot submit to the authority of his pastor or spiritual leader is dangerous as a partner. Be willing to be guided so you will not crash your home.

FOUR

MAKING YOUR
MARRIAGE BETTER

FOUR

MAKING YOUR MARRIAGE BETTER

"Make a tree good and its fruit will be good..."
(Matthew 12:33) (NIV)

Everybody prays for a good marriage and everyone desires a good home. Yet, a good home does not just happen; it is made. Good marriages are neither inherited nor awarded; they are built with a lot of wisdom and effort.

Rest assured, though; despite the alarming rates of divorce all around us, it is very possible to build a lasting marriage. My wife and I celebrated 33 years of marriage and 40 years of friendship, this past February, and it has been a beautiful experience. Of course, "Rome was not built in a day," and we did not get to where we are, overnight. However, it has been a worthwhile journey. By making daily decisions that will strengthen our bond, we have been - and remain - committed to the journey.

This is the mindset with which you make your marriage work. You must be determined to make a resounding success of it. You must give it whatever it takes, as guided by God's word. Nehemiah 4:14 says, "After I looked things over, I stood up and said to the nobles, the officials and the rest of the people, 'Don't be afraid of them. Remember the Lord, who is great and awesome, and fight for your families, your sons and your daughters, your wives and your homes'" (NIV). That is the attitude with which you build an enviable marriage.

The fact that your marriage was ordained by God does not mean that there will be no battles or challenges; neither does it mean that you will have no responsibilities. You cannot leave the success of your marriage entirely to God, without resolving to work hand-in-hand with Him, making the necessary sacrifices along the way. This means that your marriage is not about your slight happiness, but about making commitments till death do you and your spouse part. In fact, as it is in the above scripture verse, the understanding that you have God's backing in your home should propel you to believe in its success and work towards it daily.

REQUIREMENTS FOR A SUCCESSFUL MARRIAGE

1. A FIRM FOOTING ON GOD'S WORD

Although most people think that the foundation of marital success is love between the couple, it is not. Love is important; however, the number one factor that guarantees success in all areas of life, including marriage, is a sincere commitment to God's word. Love and every other attribute become easier to practice when the pillar of God's word is firmly in place.

The Psalmist says in Psalm 119:105; "Your word is a lamp to my feet And a light to my path." God's word has the power to lighten our burdens and brighten our homes. When the two persons in a marital union are absolutely submissive to the principles in God's word and committed to honoring it in their personal lives, their marriage will be indestructible.

Christ gives a confirmation of this in Matthew 7:24-27, "Therefore whoever hears these sayings of Mine, and does them, I will liken him to a wise man who built his house on the rock: and the rain descended, the floods came, and the winds blew and beat on that house; and it did not fall, for it was founded on the rock. But everyone who hears these sayings of Mine, and does not do them, will be like a foolish man who built his house on the sand: and the rain descended, the floods came, and the winds blew and beat on that house; and it fell. And great was its fall."

From this scripture, we can deduce that the secret of both marital success and marital failure is in one's attitude to God's word. Note that commitment to God's word is not just about quoting the Bible, or hearing or even preaching the word. Beyond having a sound knowledge of the word, you must live the word, being absolutely obedient to it.

The root cause of most, if not all the problems in marriages and lives, is a deviation from the word of God. This deviation is often caused by carnality and conformity to the world. It is for this reason that Apostle Paul said, "And so, dear brothers and sisters, I plead with you to give your bodies to God because of all he has done for you. Let them be a living and holy sacrifice – the kind he will find acceptable. This is truly the way to worship him. Don't copy the behavior and customs of this world, but let God transform you into a new person by changing the way you think. Then you will learn to know God's will for you, which is good and pleasing and perfect" (Romans 12:1-2) (NLT).

How many Christian couples pay attention to the above admonition? Most of the time, our ideas and expectations about marriage are copied directly from the world. We wrongly assume, like the people of the world, that the guidelines for building a successful home as described in God's word are "archaic," and not in tune with the "realities of modern life." This is why many marriages cannot withstand the test of time.

Our success in marriage and other life endeavors does not depend on emulating the ways of the world. The worldly system may seem pleasant to the flesh, but the end is often regrettable. Let your decisions in your home be reflective of your faith in Christ.

2. UNCONDITIONAL LOVE AND ACCEPTANCE

Marriage succeeds when both partners love each unconditionally. When they love each other for reasons that have nothing to do with performance, physique or achievements. If your love is based on transient things like performance, then it would mean that the day your spouse does not perform to your expectations, he or she will not be loved. This is not the kind of love that sustains a marriage. The love that solidifies a marriage is one that is rooted in the understanding that love for one's spouse is a command from God. It is not the love that is regulated by the other person's actions and attitude.

If you love your spouse because God says so, then it is a done deal. What further helps this unconditional love to grow is your acceptance of your spouse as a gift from God to you, despite his or her imperfections. When you and your spouse accept each other as gifts from God, then you will love and respect each other, and you will carry each other along in all you do. Your spouse's inadequacies or whatever it is you wish was different about them (weight, eating habits, attitude to personal hygiene, etc.), can all be addressed with love and respect, once there is acceptance.

3. COMMITMENT AND SECURITY

Marriage is a couple's covenant commitment to God and to each other; therefore, our focus and interest in all we think and do, must never be about "me," but about "us." This will require that you inconvenience yourself sometimes, in order to please your spouse. More importantly, it will require practical and intentional acts to demonstrate your commitment. The Scripture specifically says that "…a man shall leave his father and mother…" (Genesis 2:24). This is intentional and requires determination. You must be accountable for your time, your treasures, and yourself.

Marriage also thrives when each of the partners has a sense of stability, knowing that they are needed, respected, appreciated and irreplaceable. This is what security means. It has nothing to do with money; rather, it has its roots in spousal predictability or consistency of character. It means being assured of your spouse's faithfulness, loyalty and support, always.

Security in marriage entails providing a covering for your spouse, such that their inadequacies neither become a burden to them nor become exposed to other people. The Scripture says of the first couple that despite being naked, they were not ashamed - because nobody was belittling or body-shaming the other. This also underscores the power of the words we speak to our spouse. Such words can either boost or crush their self-esteem and sense of security.

Elkanah, the husband of Hannah, provides a good example for us. He was exceptionally sensitive and compassionate towards the physical and emotional needs of Hannah. He did all he could to ensure that she did not feel inferior or inadequate, despite her inability to conceive. 1 Samuel 1:4-8 says, "And whenever the time came for Elkanah to make an offering, he would give portions to Peninnah his wife and to all her sons and daughters. But to Hannah he would give a double portion, for he loved Hannah, although the LORD had closed her womb. And her rival also provoked her severely, to make her miserable, because the LORD had closed her womb. So it was, year by year, when she went up to the house of the LORD, that she provoked her; therefore she wept and did not eat. Then Elkanah her husband said to her, "Hannah, why do you weep? Why do you not eat? And why is your heart grieved? Am I not better to you than ten sons?"

Elkanah was a very good manager of his home. He operated in discernment of the Spirit by ministering peace to his brokenhearted wife. He offered his wife a covering; he served as an encourager, a builder and a comforter, instead of a deserter. Accordingly, commitment is a powerful pillar that strengthens and upholds a marriage in all circumstances.

4. Loving Communication and Crisis Management

Since communication is one of the most crucial determinants of the success of a marriage, a separate chapter has been created for it. However, let me briefly say that loving communication, whether verbal or non-verbal, is one that is expressed with the goal of fostering peace, harmony, and progress in the home. It focuses on what is right and not who is right.

Loving communication involves discussing with the purpose of agreeing. It is not about arguing - unless the argument is geared towards reaching an agreement. This kind of communication is very important because there is unlimited power when we are in agreement. Jesus, in Matthew 18:19, says, "Again I say to you that if two of you agree on earth concerning anything that they ask, it will be done for them by My Father in heaven."

This means that you can get God to move in your home, finances, career, and every other area of your life, if you and your spouse can communicate to agree. Such agreement may not fully favor your point of view but it indicates that you are both willing to bend for the sake of unity and harmony.

Unsurprisingly, communication plays a role in conflict resolution, because communication is often the cause and cure for most conflicts in the home. A healthy marriage is one that understands how to prevent and manage crisis. Ephesians 4:26-27 counsels, "Be angry, and do not sin":

do not let the sun go down on your wrath, nor give place to the devil."

This indicates that the Lord Himself knows that crisis is always a possibility in relationships. Therefore, He advocates caution. Indeed, if a couple can devise a way of initiating and handling confrontations effectively, no crisis can sink them. Confrontation is sometimes necessary because repressed discontentment will gradually lead to resentment. Therefore, learn to confront in a non-threatening way because without a confrontation, there may never be a resolution.

5. UNDERSTANDING AND NURTURING CONNECTION POINTS

In every blissful marriage, the couple often places a high value on activities that bond them. Every marriage has either of two destinations – to become stronger or to gradually break down. The reason many couples grow apart is because they nurture their differences, rather than seeking and cherishing their points of connection. The reality is that even if a marriage was solemnized in heaven, it still involves two individuals with varied interests and preferences. However, finding and cherishing points of connection is crucial to every marriage.

Sometimes you find a wife or a husband enjoying the company of a friend that the spouse does not know much about; or, either spouse is usually engrossed with certain hobbies or activities that their partner does not enjoy. If this continues and as time passes, they realize that they have little or nothing in common. This inevitably heralds a crisis and/or potential breakdown of the marriage

Therefore, no matter what your individual interests are,

you and your spouse must establish multiple connection points - things that will cause you to bond and blend more. My wife and I have many things in common and otherwise. For instance, she likes to sleep with the lights and television on. I was brought up to shut the light off when sleeping. Also, while she loves comedies, I love action movies. But we like one thing equally - cowboy movies. So, we create time to watch them together. And most importantly, we both love God and the assignment He has given to us.

The intricacies of your marriage may be unique, but all marriage partners must consciously seek to be a part of each other's world on a daily basis, for the purpose of strengthening your connection. Connection is necessary for stability and longevity. I know that we live in a world in which maintaining connection in family life is increasingly difficult. Working patterns which require a husband or wife to leave home in the early hours to go to work, often returning after the family members have gone to bed, may have an impact on family dynamics to the degree that connection and therefore, stability, are adversely affected. Efforts must be made to ensure that multiple points of connection are established and developed. Such efforts include sharing experiences together - traveling together, going on holidays together, and so on.

Other examples of connection points are family devotion time and family meal times. My wife and I used to play the scrabble game when our children were young and we were not in the ministry. John Maxwell described this as the 101 principle; having one thing that you both enjoy and giving it 100% of your energy.

61

Even in raising your children, you must be careful not to devote all of your time and attention to them at the expense of your spouse. The fact is, you knew your spouse before you had your children, and when they are grown and choose to leave home, you will still be left with your spouse. If you have allowed the children to create a disconnect between the two of you, then what happens when they are gone?

6. CREATE A POSITIVE ENVIRONMENT

Your marriage and home will be fruitful when the atmosphere is devoid of negativity and criticism. Negativity is toxic and the spirit of criticism can be very repulsive. In fact, for us to have access to the presence of God, the Scripture counsels in Psalms 100:4 that we should, "Enter into His gates with thanksgiving, And into His courts with praise…"

God's heart is open to someone who approaches Him positively in praise and thanksgiving. Since we were created in God's image, we unsurprisingly, open our hearts to those who are positive, and close our hearts to those who are negative. A person's spirit opens up when praised and closes when criticized. Within the family, we need to be each other's cheerleaders. Husbands need to root for their wives and wives for their husbands.

It is natural to gravitate towards those who affirm us. This is why the home needs to have an affirming atmosphere. Ephesians 4:29 (NLT) shows us how this works: "Don't use foul or abusive language. Let everything you say be good and helpful, so that your words will be an encouragement to those who hear them." In a home with a positive atmosphere, the husband can not wait to arrive at home, because that is where he is affirmed and built up. The wife can not wait to see her husband because she knows he is going to build her up and say loving things to her.

We need to make praise a lifestyle, beginning with praising the Lord, and doing same to each other. Even when there is a need for complaint or correction, it must be done in a loving and constructive manner. This will require the decision to never use derogatory language on each other. My wife and I made that decision a long time ago to never use any derogatory language, no matter the situation.

7. NURTURE A SAFE ATMOSPHERE FOR OPEN SHARING

A healthy marriage is a safe place to share one's heart. Such a home is a sanctuary where there is consistency in the expression of sincere concern, making each person worthy of trust.

Your spouse and children need to know that they can share anything with you and knowing that shared information will never be used against them in the future. Creating an atmosphere that is safe for open sharing requires that you eliminate all distractions that hinder meaningful conversations. For instance, when someone says he or she needs to talk to you, turn off the cell phone or TV and give that person your undivided attention. Also, when the person is done speaking, be careful and considerate in your response.

A safe atmosphere is one that communicates to your family that they are more special than the TV, work, friends, games, or anything else. When people in your family know that you are approachable and you are a good listener, the home becomes a safe haven with a loving atmosphere, where conversations will flow, effortlessly.

8. ROMANCE AND FUN

Romance is not the same as sex, but it certainly contributes to making sex feel more natural. Romance is the outward demonstration of the love you share with your spouse. It encompasses the words, thoughts, actions, and everything else that a couple does daily to show that they love and care deeply about each other. Essentially, it is the expression of passion which leads to intimate fulfillment.

At a higher and more practical level however, romance involves speaking your spouse's language of love. There are five love languages, each of which communicates love more to an individual than the others. All of the languages are nevertheless important to enhance romance and fun in the home. They include words of affirmation, acts of service, giving of gifts, spending quality time together, and engaging in playful and meaningful physical touch.

Each love language not only helps to keep romance ablaze in your home, but will also make marriage a fun experience for you. You need to consciously know your spouse's love language so you can "speak" it, as often as possible.

9. ALTAR OF CONTINUOUS FASTING AND PRAYER

No venture ever succeeds in God's Kingdom without prayer. This is especially true of marriage. Right from the beginning and to date, marriage has always been a battleground because Satan is interested in the outcomes, as well. Knowing the immense power that every couple wields once they are in accord, he uses all sorts of devices and opportunities to cause confusion, misunderstanding, and crisis in the home. This is why a couple must give themselves to prayer and fasting, individually and jointly.

1 Peter 5:8 counsels; "Be sober, be vigilant; because your adversary the devil walks about like a roaring lion, seeking whom he may devour." The enemy is not only seeking individual lives to devour but also homes to destroy. With fervent prayers however, his devices are disappointed.

Beyond keeping the evil one at bay, prayer and fasting also help to dismantle foundational strongholds that might not have been detected during the period of courtship. As already noted, there is greater power in collective prayer of agreement. This works faster to demolish every foundational barrier that may want to contend with your peace and joy in the home.

In addition, regular prayer in the family will help to strengthen the bond between a couple. The saying is indeed true that a family that prays together, stays together. It is therefore very important to intentionally set times to pray together. You can take a certain day of the week to fast and pray intentionally for your family. You will use such moments to present to God the vision and aspirations of your family.

10. FOSTERING INTIMACY

This should be the ultimate goal of every other marital pillar you erect in your home. There are four levels of intimacy - spiritual, emotional, physical and mental – with five divine laws governing them. Fostering a sense of closeness in the home requires a combination of all of these four levels and their corresponding laws. These laws as described in Genesis 2:24-25 (KJV), are:

- The law of priority. This requires that you value and prioritize your relationship above every other human relationship. "Therefore shall a man leave his father and his mother…" Love is measured by what you are willing to give up for your spouse. If you want to foster intimacy, the first thing you and your partner need to do is to give each other undivided attention. Stay away from anything or anyone that can hinder your intimacy. Be deliberate in making each other a priority. As a matter of fact, after God, your spouse is the next most important person in your life; not your job, and not your children.

- The law of intentional pursuit. "…and shall cleave unto his wife…" To "cleave" means to grab with force. It requires a decision to intentionally give your marital relationship all it takes, to achieve its intended purpose. To pursue means to intentionally engage in actions that will facilitate your bonding together as a couple and as a family. You only possess what you pursue. Every good marriage is a result of intentional daily pursuit of each other.

- The law of partnership. "…and they shall be one flesh." Marriage is a partnership. There must be no disproportionate control. If you are selfish or domineering, it will lead to problems. Have a mindset of mutual love, respect and friendship. Do not see your spouse as your competitor or as your subordinate. The word of God calls husband and wife EQUAL PARTNERS in 1 Peter 3:7 (NLT). "In the same way, you husbands must give honor to your wives. Treat your wife with understanding as you live together. She may be weaker than you are, but she is your equal partner in God's gift of new life. Treat her as you should so your prayers will not be hindered."

- The law of trust. "And they were both naked, the man and his wife, and were not ashamed." Adam and Eve were without shame because they trusted each other. Create an atmosphere of trust. This requires you to:
  o Give your spouse the right to express his or her mind - even if it is to make a complaint. Whenever you allow your spouse to express his or her dissatisfaction or pain, it builds trust in the relationship.
  o Maintain confidentiality: No secret shared in the marriage will be used against the other or shared among friends and family members. It is sacred.

- The law of transparency. Transparency is showing your spouse your true, authentic self. This includes sharing your deepest secrets and highest aspirations. This kind of transparency, when shared between two people who dutifully keep each other's sacred trust, leads to the greatest kind of intimacy. It gives the marriage partners the opportunity to be there for each other through all the trials and triumphs of life.

FIVE

ARE WE COMPATIBLE
AT ALL?

FIVE

ARE WE COMPATIBLE AT ALL?

"Let nothing be done through selfish ambition or conceit, but in lowliness of mind let each esteem others better than himself."

(Philippians 2:3)

It gives God great delight to see us enjoy every aspect of our lives, including our marriage. 3 John 1:2 (KJV) says, "Beloved, I wish above all things that thou mayest prosper and be in health, even as thy soul prospereth." Since God wants us to have marital success, He has made the necessary provisions for this to be actualized. All we need to do is abide by His blueprint and we will have a blissful home.

One of God's provisions is the assignment of roles to each of the parties that make up the Christian marriage – the husband and the wife. Interestingly, in assigning these roles, God has taken careful consideration of the way He has wired each gender. God has the best understanding of our fundamental needs, desires, expectations, and motivators, as men and women. To ensure that those needs are met, He has revealed to both husbands and wives what they must do individually, to make their marriage work.

Before discussing the roles, it is important to understand and appreciate the differences in the genders. We must be reminded again that God made humans male and female – both physiologically and psychologically – and both genders are said to be made in the image of God. This means that both men and women are as God intended them to be. It would therefore be unrealistic, or even unreasonable, to expect our spouses to think, feel, act and react, exactly as we do.

That said, it must also be emphasized that rigidity has no place in a home governed by love and guided by the dictates of God's word. Each gender can learn to "bend" their nature where necessary, to ensure peace, harmony, and progress in the home. This is why 1 Peter 3:7 speaks of "understanding."

One of the major sources of friction in marriage is the inability or the refusal to dwell with each other with understanding. I can comfortably say that I understand my wife and she understands me. I know what to do to make my wife joyful or tearful. I know what to do to make her smile or cry. I know what to do to make her fulfilled or unfulfilled. As a Christian husband who wants a joyful home, I simply continue to do the good things that will make her joyful, smile and fulfilled.

Understanding does not mean that your spouse will always do things in a way that pleases you; but there will always be the willingness to adapt, as motivated by love, on both sides. Compatibility, then, does not necessarily mean that there will be no differences between the two of you; it only means that you have a balanced attitude or set of ideas and principles that help you to live together, happily.

GENDER DIFFERENCES

As previously mentioned, knowing some of the differences between the male and the female genders will help us to understand what drives their expectations, as well as why God has assigned different roles to marriage partners.

Due to the differences in the way the male and female brains are wired, as well as the primary hormones secreted in their bodies (testosterone for men and estrogen for women), men and women tend to have different behavioral patterns, priorities, inclinations, and preferences. For instance, while men generally tend to be more action-oriented and adventurous, finding greater joy and fulfilment in accomplishments, women are more reflective and find greater joy and fulfilment in the richness of their relationships. Unlike men, women appreciate intimacy more than action. Again, while women tend to think more broadly, men tend to think more deeply.

Other noticeable differences between the genders are:

1. While men are target-oriented, with the eagerness to move from one action to another, according to their "timetable" or "deadlines," women are more reflective of the long-range impact of the actions. Women are more relaxed; they take time to enjoy every moment. You can understand this better when you consider the way men and women approach sex. While men want

to go straight to "the act," women place a very high value on foreplay and afterplay. While men ascend and descend the peak of passion very quickly, both take a much longer time for women. And while men want to quickly move on after the action, women want to spend more time cuddling and savoring the moment.

2. Since men are more of "doers," they pay less attention to people's feelings and in the process of striving to meet their goals, could sacrifice social life and important connections. Women on the other hand, place more value on caring for others and connecting with them on so many levels.

3. Men tend to talk just to communicate information and ideas, while women use words to communicate their thoughts and feelings. This means that most times men do not talk, until they consider it necessary.

4. While men are more adventurous, women tend to value security and safety, and consequently tend to be more careful and reserved.

Of course, there are many more differences such as how men and women input, process and deliver information; but those listed above should facilitate your understanding of why aspirations and expectations in relationships tend to differ between men and women.

EXPECTATIONS OF MEN

What does a man expect from his wife?

- Respect. Men want their wives to respect them as the head of the family. Nothing provokes a man to better performance like appreciation and respect.

They would love to be addressed politely by their wives.

- Men want their wives to be soft-spoken and not foul-mouthed, and to always seek their opinion on issues, before crucial decisions are made. They do not want their wives to be "Mrs. Know-It-All."

- Men appreciate women that are gentle in approaching their weaknesses for correction, instead of trying to effect change, forcibly. Men do not like domineering wives that will impose rules and orders.

- Men appreciate women who respect them by being faithful to the marital covenant and by not keeping company with friends and relatives that give bad advice or have a negative influence.

- Men love wives that encourage them. This motivates them to pursue and achieve their goals. I am eternally grateful for my wife's words of affirmation during the days of struggle. She was always there with kind words of reassurance. Nothing makes a man strong and motivated like the encouraging words of his wife, especially when the man is still struggling. A good wife is a cheerleader. Men perform better when they have people cheering them. Cheerleaders celebrate everything, no matter how little the success. Do not let the devil focus your mind on what your husband is doing wrong; look for a reason to praise and respect him. Men gravitate to where they receive honor and recoil from where there is no honor. Cheerleaders also find positive ways of saying negative things.

As a woman, you have the power in your mouth to make your husband what he should become.

- Men love wives that have a vision, so they can assist in actualizing their vision. Women without a vision, plan, or goals slow down the progress of their husbands.

- Men delight in wives that are contented with the little they can afford at a time. They are happy with women who help in sharing the financial burden in the home.

- Men expect their wives to satisfy their sexual urges, always. Women who deny their husbands sex invite trouble into the marriage.

- Men are moved by what they see and as such a wife is expected to be neat and presentable at all times.

- Men appreciate women who are good home-makers. They want a wife who is concerned about the home being tidy and inviting, as well as the family having good nutrition.

Here is an interesting illustration on pleasing a husband. A woman seeking counsel from Dr. George W. Crane, the psychologist, confided that she hated her husband, and intended to divorce him. "I want to hurt him all I can," she declared firmly. "Well, in that case," said Dr. Crane, "I advise you to start showering him with compliments. When you have become indispensable to him, when he thinks you love him devotedly, then start the divorce action. That is the way to hurt him." Some months later the wife returned to report that all was going well. She had followed the suggested course. "Good," said Dr. Crane. "Now's the time to file for divorce." "Divorce!" the woman said indignantly. "Never. I love my husband dearly!"

EXPECTATIONS OF WOMEN

D.L. Moody once said, "If I want to find out whether a man is a Christian, I would not go to a minister; I would go and ask his wife. If a man does not treat his wife right, I do not want to hear him talk about Christianity. What is the use of talking about salvation for the next life if he has no salvation for this life?"

What exactly do women want in a relationship or marriage? This has been the subject of debates from time immemorial. The story is often told of a man who was walking along a California beach and stumbled across an old lamp. He picked it up and rubbed it and out popped a genie. The genie said, "Okay, you released me from the lamp. This is the fourth time this month and I am getting a little sick of these wishes so you can forget about three. You only get one wish!"

The man sat and thought about it for a while and said, "I have always wanted to go to Hawaii but I am scared to fly and I get very seasick. Could you build me a bridge to Hawaii so I can drive over there to visit?" The genie laughed and said, "That is impossible. Think of the logistics of that! How would the supports ever reach the bottom of the Pacific? Think of how much concrete... how much steel!! No, think of another wish."

The man said, "Okay," and tried to think of a really good wish. Finally, he said, "I have been married and divorced four times. My wives always said that I do not care and that I am insensitive. So, I wish that I could understand women – to know how they feel inside and what they are thinking when they give me the silent treatment; to know why they are crying; to know what they really want when they say 'nothing'; to know how to make them truly happy...." The genie cut in, "Do you want that bridge with two lanes or four?"

The above is one of the jokes often used to highlight how difficult it can be for some men to understand what women generally want. But your wife is not just part of the general population of women; she is your wife and therefore, it is very much possible to know her likes and dislikes. In fact, it is your duty to know them.

Even if you are not married yet, you can have an idea of what a wife – and especially a Christian wife – would expect of her husband. These include:

- Security. This is the number one need of a woman. Men are honor-oriented, while women are security-oriented. Security is the state of being protected or safe from harm. It means freedom from risk or danger; freedom from doubt, anxiety or fear. Your wife must feel safe and protected with you always. She must have the assurance that you are absolutely committed to her and have her best interest at heart always. Indeed, what makes a woman most secure is a selfless and sacrificial man. Women are insecure when they are married to a selfish, detached husband who is not in tune with them. Your wife must be the priority in your life, after God.

- Faithfulness and honesty. These two qualities may seem similar, but they are not exactly the same. Faithfulness is defined as being true to your vows, words, and promises. It means being trustworthy and dependable. Honesty, on the other hand means refusing to lie, cheat, or deceive in any way; it simply means truthfulness. Faithfulness and truthfulness are absolutes if you want to enjoy your wife.

- Leadership ability. Women cherish a man who demonstrates leadership competencies in providing guidance and direction for the family. However, this leading must be done with kindness and understanding, and with the consideration/inclusion of the wife's ideas and contributions.

- Love/affection. This is not the same as sex or sexual passion. The definition of love to a woman is tender affection and personal attachment. The biblical definition for this kind of love is "agape" (unconditional) love. Such love encompasses knowing and understanding your wife and meeting her at the point of her need.

- Listening ability. Men are known to be good talkers but bad listeners. Sometimes, what your wife needs is for you to just listen. Do not interrupt; let her unburden her heart. The best way for a woman to "reset" is sometimes by getting all of her thoughts out. Let your wife talk through her feelings and problems. Show empathy. Listen carefully. Ask questions. Be fully engaged in the conversation. Do not trash her words and opinions. Let her know that her words and views are very important to you. You may not even agree with her viewpoint; but there is a way you compose responses and gestures that will make her relax and be at peace.

- Purposeful living. Women love men who are hard-working and purpose-driven. Laziness, indecision, and the inability to provide the basic needs of the home are huge turn-offs for most women.

- True partnership. Most men do fall into the "teaching trap" when they are supposed to be a partner, showing love and consideration. Do not blame your wife, just be there for her. If she wants you to offer solutions, she will ask for them.

- Sensitivity to her needs. Get to know your wife's moods and needs. Endeavor to know what is needed to be done for her and do them without being prompted. Learn the art of anticipating her needs and meeting them without being asked. What is broken that needs to be fixed? Do not wait to be asked. Just do it!

- Appreciation/affirmation. Your wife loves to know that she means the world to you. She wants to know you cherish, value and appreciate her. You can do this through your words and your actions. Spend quality time with her. Pay attention to her dressing, hairdo and other things she does to look good for you. Take her out to places she loves. Buy her gifts. And above all, make it a point of duty to frequently compliment her. Let her know in all the ways you can say or write it, that she is beautiful and that you really do love her. Compliment her when she does anything around the house no matter how small it is. My wife and I always say that we will never take each other for granted. Do not take what your wife does in the house for granted. If your wife cooks or makes the bed, learn to say, "thank you honey."

- Health and hygiene. Just as you want your wife to look neat, good, and fit, so also does she want you to take the issues of your health and personal hygiene seriously. No woman will be comfortable with a man who cannot clean up after himself or make the effort to look and smell great for his woman.

- Vulnerability. Women want men who can loosen up a bit, once in a while, to let them know your fears, worries and concerns. It does not in any way connote weakness on your part; it only shows that you are human and that you trust her enough to confide in her.

While the above list of gender differences and expectations may not be exhaustive, what matters most is the desire to make your marriage work. Once that exists, it will be easy to study, observe, and understand what makes your spouse unique and what causes him or her to be happy and to feel loved.

SIX

FULFILLING YOUR MARITAL ROLES

SIX
FULFILLING YOUR MARITAL ROLES

"Wives, submit to your own husbands, as to the Lord. For the husband is head of the wife, as also Christ is head of the church...Husbands, love your wives, just as Christ also loved the church and gave Himself for her..."

(Ephesians 5:22-25)

God's perfect plan for an indestructible marriage is found in the Bible, and if this plan is followed wholeheartedly, marriages would be blissful. God never creates anything to fail, or to hurt or frustrate us. The reason why some marriages are experiencing challenges today is because people are trying to do things in their own way or according to worldly principles. The roles and responsibilities of a husband and wife in an indestructible marriage can be found in Ephesians 5:22-33, which states:

"Wives, submit to your own husbands, as to the Lord. For the husband is head of the wife, as also Christ is head of the church; and He is the Savior of the body. Therefore, just as the church is subject to Christ, so let the wives be to their own husbands in everything. Husbands, love your wives, just as Christ also loved the church and gave Himself for her that He might sanctify and cleanse her with the washing of water by the word, that He might present her to Himself a glorious church, not having spot or wrinkle or any such thing, but that she should be holy and without blemish. So husbands ought to love their own wives as their own bodies; he who loves his wife loves himself. For no one ever hated his own flesh, but nourishes and cherishes it, just as the Lord does the church. For we are members of His body, of His flesh and of His bones. "For this reason a man shall leave his father and mother and be joined to his wife, and the two shall become one flesh." This is a great mystery, but I speak concerning Christ and the church. Nevertheless let each one of you in particular so love his own wife as himself, and let the wife see that she respects her husband."

There are usually two unhelpful reactions to the above scriptural guidelines for marital success, which must be avoided.

- The first is the tendency to ignore what is expected of you, while focusing on your spouse's roles.

- The second is the tendency to accept that we actually do have roles to play, but we refuse to make the first move. Some men wonder why they should love a woman who is not submissive, while some women say they will only submit to their husband as unto the Lord, when he behaves like the Lord.

The truth, however, is that we need not feel intimidated by these divine prescriptions. God will not prescribe medications that have side-effects. Embracing the roles in Ephesians Chapter 5 will make you more attractive to your spouse and will cause his or her heart to be more open to you. Simply put, these divine principles will also showcase your spouse's amazing potential. In essence, no one will lose in a marriage that honors God.

When God asks the woman to be submissive to the husband and the man to love his wife, it is meant to subdue the inherent sinful nature that is unique to men and women.

What is the relational sin nature of women? The desire to be independent. Genesis 3:6 (NLT) says, "The woman was convinced. She saw that the tree was beautiful and its fruit looked delicious, and she wanted the wisdom it would give her. So she took some of the fruit and ate it. Then she gave some to her husband, who was with her, and he ate it, too."

We know that the devil went to Eve and tempted her in the Garden of Eden. She entered into a conversation with Satan, when all she needed to do was to slow down, turn to Adam, and seek direction on how to handle the devil. Many married women think they have within them all that they need to be independent. They believe that they know it all, or are more spiritual and do not need their husband's leadership. This is how many end up making avoidable mistakes.

What is the sin nature of men? It is the negligence of their duties of care and protection towards their wives. God commanded Adam to subdue every creeping thing on the earth. To subdue means to subjugate; to bring under control. Unfortunately, Adam was nowhere to be found, when a creeping thing (serpent) began to speak to his wife about rebelling against God. Adam was not there for the wife when she needed him the most. This is how the sin nature destroys a marriage.

In Ephesians 5, God places an obligation on the woman to be accountable. Treat your husband and his counsel like you would that of the Lord (Ephesians 5:22). On the other hand, God instructs men to deeply and genuinely love their wives. Such love is active, not passive. It manifests in sacrificial giving, showing genuine concern and interest for her, and being consistently supportive. Elkanah in 1 Samuel 1:4-8, was there for his wife at all times - to protect her, to care for her, to safeguard her self-esteem, and to provide for her needs.

The godly role of a man is to bring the wife to her full potential. A husband should be asking, "Why did God create my wife?" "Is it to be a stay-at-home mom, a worship leader, a teacher, etc.?" He should then see himself as God's partner to help her become who God created her to be. You are to help your wife in accomplishing her goals. Every man will stand before God one day to give an account of the most important thing He ever gave you - your wife. Are you God's partner or Satan's partner?

A good way to know your wife's purpose is to ask her what God has placed in her heart to become. Then, pray about it. You will help her fulfil her purpose through nurture, prayer, caring, and so on. A good husband is a greenhouse that provides a good environment where the wife can grow and become all she can be.

Your wife reflects your nurture and character. The woman

is the glory of the husband. Women are transformed and find fulfilment in the atmosphere of security, while men find fulfilment in the atmosphere of honor.

SPECIFIC MARITAL ROLES

The specific roles of marriage partners as advocated in Ephesians 5, can be deemed to be the five-fold ministries of husbands and wives.

THE HUSBAND

- Protect. It is your responsibility as a husband, to protect your wife. Protection involves sacrificing your life for your wife's, if need be. It is making your wife's wellbeing of prime importance by protecting and caring for her as you would your own body. Of course, God Himself is our ultimate protector; but it is your ministry to prevent certain things from happening to your wife. For example, it is your duty to defend your wife against your family's harassment or interference in your home.

- Provide. Irrespective of the state of the economy or the society you live in, it is very paramount to provide for your wife. Even when you are both working, look out for your wife and be generous to her. According to Genesis 2:15, "Then the LORD God took the man and put him in the Garden of Eden to tend and keep it." Similarly, 1 Timothy 5:8 states; "But if anyone does not provide for his own, and especially for those of his household, he has denied the faith and is worse than an unbeliever." Therefore, being gainfully employed is a must for a husband.

- Prefer. Always look out for your wife. Apart from God, let her be your number one in everything you do. Prefer your wife over the children; over your friends; over your family members; and over your hobbies. Let it be clearly known to people that you do not joke with your wife. Give your wife the best, every time.

- Present. You present your wife unto yourself by the washing of the word. Make your wife what you want her to be, in alignment with God's purpose for your lives. Expose her to the word of God. Expose her to the right utterances from you. Expose her to grace through prayer. Take time off to pray for her. Hand her over to her Maker, who knows the deepest need of her heart. Let God fix her; you cannot do it. Ask God to teach you how you can be a better spouse to her. Ask Him to comfort her and help her see herself as He sees her. Do not just pray for her; pray with her. Find the time. Hug her or hold her hands as you pray together.

- Permit. Allow your wife to shine. Only cowardly men do not allow their wives to shine. Teach your wife to grow and do exploits. Permit her to express herself, which will require you to be secure in yourself. Discover and embrace your wife's uniqueness.

THE WIFE

- **Submit.** It is biblical. As far as submission and respect are concerned, your number one loyalty is to your own husband. The greatest need of a man is respect, not sex or food. Some women are more submissive to other men than to their husbands. They are submissive to their bosses, doctors, lawyers, and pastors, but not to their husbands. An example of submission is consulting your husband before taking major decisions. Read Genesis 3:6 again; "And when the woman saw that the tree was good for food, and that it was pleasant to the eyes, and a tree to be desired to make one wise, she took of the fruit thereof, and did eat, and gave also unto her husband with her; and he did eat." Unfortunately, the absence of submission led to the Fall.

In addition, when you disrespect your husband, you are disrespecting your destiny. God hates it. It is a sign of pride and immaturity. Respect him, whether in private or public. There is a way you relate to your husband that will cause others to respect him. For example, irrespective of who you are with on a phone call, when your husband gets home, you must pause and honor him. Validate your husband; let him know that he is important to you.

- **Serve.** Being married goes beyond a change of status. It is also acceptance of responsibilities that are naturally that of the woman. Taking care of the home and the children, for example, are better handled by a woman, being a natural nurturer – even though a good husband is supposed to render all necessary assistance.

- **Support.** Nothing develops and brings a man to total manhood than a supportive wife. Support is rendered, firstly, with your utterances to him.

Secondly, support him with your actions. For example, a supportive wife will put food on the table if need be, without rubbing it in her husband's face. Be a reliable support system for your husband. A support system undergirds and helps to keep stable. There is no man a woman cannot make, and there is no husband a woman cannot destroy. Within every husband is a king that wants to reign. Do all you can to support your husband and sustain your home, in all circumstances. Do not give room to complaints. Get to know your husband's state of mind at all times; know when to speak and not to speak, and of course, when to provide the necessary support.

- **Seduce.** Every man wants a woman that is neat and presentable. Some women look good when going out but dress shabbily indoors. Look good in the house. That you have children is not an excuse to look haggard around your husband.

Look good and smell good for your man. Put away worn-out night wears and tattered hairnets. Become unpredictable for him. Change the styles of your hair, clothing, and even undies, unexpectedly. Men are moved by sight and love variety. Since your born-again husband cannot have extramarital affairs, it is your obligation to duly engage his senses.

When your husband lovingly calls your attention to something that has to do with your looks, do not rebuff him. Be a woman of wisdom. Repackage yourself. Exercise, if you have to. You must constantly improve yourself. Every man loves variety. No matter how anointed a man is, he is affected by what he sees. You can combine spirituality with a happy home. You can be both anointed and submissive.

- **Surround** him with your watchful eyes and ears, and most importantly, with your prayers. Men naturally have issues with ego, but that should not stop you from lovingly raising issues of concern about him. Maybe he is not paying enough attention to his health. Even if he pretends not to take your concerns seriously, you still have the weapon of prayer to influence him. You are the intercessor. Men are natural hunters and women are natural warriors. Unleash the warrior in you to safeguard your man and your home.

SEVEN

MANAGING YOUR FINANCES

SEVEN

MANAGING YOUR FINANCES

"We have brought nothing into the world, so we cannot take anything out of it either"
(1 Timothy 6:7) (NASB).

This is an important area of roles and responsibilities in the home that has often generated conflicts, even in Christian marriages. Indeed, most marriage experts agree that finances can be the number one cause of marital strain. This strain is understandable because how people spend money is never just about the money - it reveals attitudes about what they value most; it reveals deeper character issues.

Usually, the foundation of money-related marital conflict is ownership of money. It should be established that, in a marriage, especially a Bible-based one, there is no "my money" and "your money" or "my debts" and "your debts." There is only "our money" and "our debts."

When God said in Genesis 2:24, "They shall become one flesh," He was referring to "flesh," in the general sense. Husband and wife must be one in everything, including their finances. A couple cannot attain oneness if they separate their finances. A marriage is not a 50/50 relationship, as many people think. It is a 100/100 relationship on both sides. Each must be willing to yield 100 percent of their rights to their spouses. If they are not willing to do that, it will not work.

Since in a marriage, a husband and wife are one, the financial assets and incomes of both husband and wife should be merged and they should operate from a unified financial management base, rather than from a separate and independent management base. God usually strengthens the bond between a couple if, from the very beginning, they establish His Word as their financial guide and then follow His principles for managing their resources.

No viable marriage can survive a "his or hers" relationship for long, because it is totally contrary to God's plan. To this end, couples must avoid having separate financial dealings, including checking accounts, because when they develop a "his money/her money" philosophy, it usually leads to a he-versus-she mentality. By and large, unwillingness to join all assets and bank accounts after marriage perhaps signals the danger that unresolved trust issues could still be lingering or developing in the relationship.

How do you jointly manage your finances and meet your needs?

There is the YOURS, MINE AND OURS, in which a couple have a common account for joint savings, while each keeps a portion of their incomes to themselves, based on mutual agreement.

There is also the FULLY OURS pattern, in which you take both of your checks, put them together, and the best money-manager manages the common account without intimidation.

There are rules that govern such a joint account.

- The first is that it is not compulsory that a man or a woman must manage the family's account. Either of you can do it, since you are partners.

- Second, there must be established allowances out of the account.

- Third, both must have access to the account.

- Fourth, there should be a serious limit on how you surprise each other. This means that there must be no major purchases from the account without agreement.

Essentially, the account must be handled with vision, selflessness, prudence, fear of God and integrity.

PRINCIPLES FOR HANDLING FINANCES

1. Acknowledge that God owns everything. "We have brought nothing into the world, so we cannot take anything out of it either" (1 Timothy 6:7) (NASB). Once couples accept the fact that God owns everything and that they have been chosen to be stewards or managers of God's property, it becomes easy for them to manage according to His principles and standards. We must be mindful that it is how we faithfully manage what He has given us that will determine whether He will give us greater things to manage. (Matthew 25:23).

2. Think ahead and avoid problems. "Which one of you, when he wants to build a tower, does not first sit

down and calculate the cost to see if he has enough to complete it?" (Luke 14:28) (NASB). Too often, couples put off planning until they are so deeply in debt that it seems impossible to get out. By then it is too late to plan, except for crisis planning. Obviously, one of the first goals is to avoid financial bondage by staying out of additional debt and committing to paying off existing debt. This does not necessarily mean that you should not borrow, but borrowing to buy consumables, such as gifts, vacations, and clothes, should be avoided. This type of spending will lead a couple into insurmountable debt, faster than they can pay their way out of it.

3. Choose what matters most. If you cannot have it all, discover the most important aspects of your activities. Figure out what brings you the greatest enjoyment. Then, look for ways to have fun without breaking the bank. What is the best thing about going to the movies? If you think it is the atmosphere, attend an earlier (cheaper) show. If you like discussing films with friends, rent one to watch at home, and invite your family friends.

4. Cherish what you have. When the Joneses are buying hot tubs and big screen TVs, it is usually tempting to pull out the credit card and keep in step. It is the American way, right? How quickly we forget to thank God for the simplest of things! Even hot showers, comfortable homes, and cabinets full of food, are luxuries to people in some other nations. Challenge yourself to take your eyes off of your neighbor's "toys" and to reflect upon your everyday blessings.

EIGHT

COMMUNICATION:
THE TONIC OF INTIMACY

EIGHT

COMMUNICATION: THE TONIC OF INTIMACY

"Let no corrupt word proceed out of your mouth, but what is good for necessary edification, that it may impart grace to the hearers."

(Ephesians 4:29)

Constructive communication is perhaps the most effective lubricant of the wheels of marriage. When a couple communicates freely, properly, and honestly, understanding flows, conflicts are easily avoided or resolved, and an atmosphere of peace and bliss envelops the home.

There is a need to emphasize constructive communication, since any conflicting form of communication will only bring contrary results to the home. And indeed, most of the crises that rattle families often result from poor communication patterns and systems. Dennis Rainey rightly explains that "authentic communication is much more than just talking. It is understanding and being understood; identifying a tone of voice; detecting nonverbal cues; responding appropriately to offense; resolving conflicts; knowing what to say, when to say it, and how to say it; experiencing the risks and rewards of knowing and being known; and much more."

DIMENSIONS OF COMMUNICATION

There are six reasons for which we communicate:

1. To exchange basic information by telling the other person what they need to know. For instance, "Honey, dinner is ready."
2. For partnership. This is done to get the other person's assistance, since you are in a partnership and cannot do it alone. For example, "Please, stop by the store on your way home."
3. For conflict resolution. This is for airing grievances.
4. For connection. Just having a good time conversing about happenings in your environment, or things that concern your home, or about life in general.
5. To provide personal information. This involves sharing of feelings, thoughts, frustrations, worries, concerns, and fears.
6. For intimacy. This is to express love, affirmation, and sexual desires.

ELEMENTS OF CONSTRUCTIVE COMMUNICATION

Constructive communication is communication that builds, uplifts, and edifies. Ephesians 4:29 counsels; "Don't use foul or abusive language. Let everything you say be good and helpful, so that your words will be an encouragement to those who hear them" (NLT). How do we achieve this as we communicate in the home? It is by paying attention to the following essential elements:

1. **The right tone.** Tone matters a lot in communication. Your tone conveys the attitude with which you are communicating. In fact, your partner will know whether you mean what you are saying or not. Your tone will either uplift or upset your spouse. What you are expressing may be true and justified, but your tone should not be abusive, disrespectful, or toxic. Do not ever try to rationalize your usage of an inappropriate tone. Regardless of how your friends speak to their spouses in your presence; regardless of what you see in the movies; regardless of how your parents spoke to each other; never sacrifice the power of a good tone when talking to your spouse.

2. **The right time.** This has to do with quality and quantity. Your conversation should be held at an appropriate time and with enough time to talk. Look at the example of Abigail in 1 Samuel 25:36-37 (KJV): "And Abigail came to Nabal; and, behold, he held a feast in his house, like the feast of a king; and Nabal's heart was merry within him, for he was very drunken: wherefore she told him nothing, less or more, until the morning light. But it came to pass in the morning, when the wine was gone out of Nabal, and his wife had told him these things..."

Nabal was in a drunken state which meant that he was not in the right frame of mind to digest what his wife had to tell him. She had to wait for a better time. It is not everything that can be said at any time. Wisdom requires that conversations - especially those that may degenerate into arguments - should be reserved for certain times, so that a positive agreement can be reached, and the likelihood of a misunderstanding can be minimized. This is the qualitative aspect of the right timing in communication.

You also need ample time to communicate. Purposefully select a suitable and sufficient timeframe. Talk sooner, so you do not have to fight later. When you are proactive in your communication, you will not be reactive. Amos 3:3 asks, "Can two walk together except they are in agreement?" You must sit down together to agree on how to manage your lives.

Setting aside enough time for personal communication is imperative. You and your spouse should be talking constantly, everyday. Talk about yourselves, your children, your jobs, your hobbies, and so on. Turn off the TV, the phone and all other distractions, especially from the social media. Also, create enough time for intimate communication. Flirt with each other - it is allowed.

3. **Atmosphere of trust.** Trust is being readdressed here, within the context of constructive communication.

There are two elements necessary for the creation of an atmosphere of trust:

- Give your spouse the right to express his or her mind - even if it is to make a complaint. Whenever you allow your spouse to express his or her dissatisfaction or pain; it builds trust in the relationship.
- Maintain confidentiality: No secret shared in the home will be used against the other or shared among friends and family members.

4. **Atmosphere of truth.** Ephesians 4:15 declares,"… speaking the truth in love…" Also as Jimmy Evans said, "truth without grace is mean and grace without truth is meaningless." Here is an interesting paradox – a relationship without conflicts is not as satisfying as the one with conflicts and loving resolutions.

5. **Team spirit.** When you become a team and respect each other, your marriage be will be indestructible. Genuine communication requires that husband and wife each seek to understand and to be understood. By so doing, they will value what it takes for genuine communication to occur.

To demonstrate team spirit in your communication, you have to be a good listener.

A good listener:

- Listens with an attitude that encourages communication. Romans 12:10.

- Gives adequate attention and priority to what the partner is saying.

- Listens with an attitude of acceptance and willingness to understand.

- Listens with the knowledge that the spouse is not the enemy.

- Listens with the willingness to hear what God may be saying through the spouse.

- Anticipates clarification. Asks questions and paraphrases statements in order to understand the true meaning of the message.

A poor listener, on the other hand, manifests habits that stifle communication and stir misunderstanding. He or she is selective in listening and only tunes in for points of interest. In fact, most bad listeners only listen to a person for the sole purpose of gathering ammunition to support their position. This is the reason most discussions with bad listeners never stay on track. This does not encourage a team spirit or effective communication in the home.

Moreover, a couple must allow freedom for differences in styles of expression. Some people have closed emotions, thereby having difficulty with expressing their feelings, while others have difficulty with minimizing or concealing their emotions.

6. **The principle of prayer.** Success in communication is more likely when we invite God to be an active participant and guide. This principle is not complicated, but it requires close attention. No matter what principle you apply or when you speak or the topic of your conversation, no scenario is beyond prayer.

Satanic opposition and pride will set in when we do not actively invite God into our relationship. R.A. Torrey said of prayer: "The reason why many fail in battle is because they wait until the hour of battle. The reason why others succeed is because they have gained their victory on their knees long before the battle... Anticipate your battles; fight them on your knees before temptation comes, and you will always have victory."

TRAITS OF DESTRUCTIVE COMMUNICATION

One of the ways we can begin to improve our family communication is by learning to identify unhealthy communication traits. These include:

1. **Malicious silence.** Rather than talking about issues and resolving them relationally, many people use silence to both punish and intimidate their spouses and families. At the first sign of tension or conflict, the healthy thing to do is to sit down and talk things out before they get out of hand. However, some people clam up and become irritable. Silence in a marriage and family is very dangerous. It is not only a non-rational, anti-social form of behavior, but it also guarantees prolonged problems.

2. **Verbal abuse.** There are two levels of verbal abuse in families. The first is between a couple - husband and wife get into a disagreement and begin to yell, scream, curse, name-call and belittle each other. This is extremely damaging for the couple themselves and also for their children. The second level is between parents and their children. Let us be reminded that our words are powerful generally, but the words we speak upon our spouses and children have even more far-reaching consequences.

3. **Manipulation.** This involves communication that is aimed at emotional blackmail and subjugation. It involves speaking in a certain way in order to deceive, confuse, or coerce your spouse to bend to your will.

4. **Erratic behavior.** This means unpredictability. One

day, the world is great, the mood is good, and positive things are being said. The next day, the mood may be bad and angry words are spoken. The spouses and children do not know what to expect in this type of home. An atmosphere of insecurity and mistrust prevails in such a volatile environment. If something is upsetting to you, do not take it out on your family members.

5. **Secrecy.** This involves hiding important information or details from your spouse for selfish reasons. This breeds mistrust and may result in embarrassment or even more serious problems for the home.

RULES FOR EDIFYING COMMUNICATION

The following suggestions will help you to promote healthy communication and avoid destructive interactions:

1. Define rules in your communication. You must know that there are things you can never say to each other. My wife and I never use derogatory words on each other, regardless of what we are discussing.
2. Wait for the right time to communicate. James 1:19.
3. Never embarrass each other publicly or before the children.
4. Passionately express yourself without making personal attacks.
5. Remain focused on the subject at hand. Do not bring in other issues.
6. Be sensitive and respectful of your differences. If he or she says it is important, then it is important. A person's perception is their reality. You should not

be rigid and must endeavor to see the other person's perspective.

7. Admit it when you are wrong.
8. Do not expect your spouse to read your mind. Speak out.
9. Give compliments.
10. Participate in a support group throughout the lifespan of your relationship. Be around people who have appreciation for marriage.

COUPLES' EXERCISE

A. Write five things your spouse does that you like and you do not want him/her to stop doing.

1.

2.

3.

4.

5.

B. Write five things your spouse does that you do not like and you want him or her to stop doing.

1.

2.

3.

4.

5.

NINE

DIVORCE-PROOFING YOUR MARRIAGE

NINE

DIVORCE-PROOFING YOUR MARRIAGE

"So then, they are no longer two but one flesh. Therefore what God has joined together, let not man separate."

(Matthew 19:6)

What is the secret to a long, happy marriage such as yours? The common answer to this question, from people in happy marriages, is "I married my best friend."

This is how interesting, enjoyable, and enduring God wants us all of our marriages to be. And since we have His backing and everything else that we need to succeed, all that is required of each of us is to purposefully ensure that our marriage is not counted among the increasing statistics of failed marriages.

All marriages have to undergo a transition from the initial thrill of romantic attraction and overwhelming sexual desire, to the stage when other things must become as or more significant. After being swept off your feet by true love, ask yourself what comes next. Will you wake up next to the same person for five or six decades and still find a person you like, as well as love? This is why it is important to marry someone that is really meant for you – a lifetime friend, the bone of your bone and the flesh of your flesh.

MUTUAL GROWTH

Another crucial observation is that successful couples learn and grow together. No one is stagnant or left to depreciate. After being married for 30 years, a couple decided that they would both return to school for a master's degree in liberal arts. I recall them saying, "It took us nearly five years. We had a great time being in class together, studying together, and reading together. The program allowed us to expand our horizons as we took courses in religion, politics, literature, history, foreign policy. We even persuaded one professor to let us write a paper together as joint authors!"

Partners in successful marriages play to each other's strengths and interests. If one partner becomes more health-conscious, the other joins. If one partner takes up a new activity, the other partner becomes supportive and involved. The end result is a stronger emotional bond and a deeper love.

AGREEMENTS TOWARDS SUCCESS

In addition to the above, you and your spouse must agree and commit yourselves to the following ideals, in order to fortify and renew your marriage, daily.

1. You must agree to build your marriage on the word of God. Your culture did not create your marriage. God is the author and the creator of marriage, and marriage partners must align with the producer of the

institution. This is why it is good to marry someone who has the same spiritual conviction as you.

2. You must agree to leave the past behind. Everybody has a past, including yourself and your spouse. Yesterday ended last night. Do not become an archaeologist in your relationship.

3. You must agree to continually work on your marriage. It is so easy to take things for granted and get stuck in the routines of daily life. When last did you buy any meaningful gift for your spouse? When last did you go on a vacation together without the children? When last did you exchange romantic messages or even had passionate sex?

4. You must both agree to change. You must agree that you both need to change. Many people believe their partners need to change, but your prayer should be for God to make you a better husband or a better wife.

5. You must agree to disagree. Do not create an atmosphere where your spouse cannot disagree with you.

6. You must agree to give 100 percent to the relationship. Tell yourself, "I am going to give it whatever it takes."

7. You must agree to be together forever. It should be your philosophy, your ethic, and your belief. "Together forever" should be your motto.

KEY REMINDERS

Finally, here are a few key reminders of the strategies for building an unbreakable marriage.

1. Ensure that your home is built on the foundation of God's word - not lust, societal demands, wealth, beauty, talents, or other carnal considerations. Both of you must be committed to living by the principles of God's word and the leading of His Spirit.

2. Establish times of fellowship together. Have a consistent time of fasting and prayer, with your relationship as the main focus.

3. Define guidelines to protect your relationship from competing affections - friends, children, career, relatives, etc.

4. Ensure that you establish a consistent communication forum. Have a day that you sit down to discuss your issues, in-depth.

5. Make yourselves accountable to an individual or entity. Join a Bible-believing and family-centered church. You should accept godly counsel and wisdom to mediate differences. Be wise enough to seek and accept the opinions of individuals whose advice you value, in instances where you cannot reach a decision or an agreement.

6. With maturity, make collective decisions and resolve to stay focused.

7. Individually maintain self-worth and self-esteem based on God, and apart from your mate. Make this a full-time assignment.

8. Establish a proven, problem-solving regimen to eliminate the feeling of being overwhelmed.

9. Stay in an atmosphere of faith that supports marriage and success. Listen to marriage relationship audio teachings and read helpful publications on a regular basis.

10. Avoid covetous competition with other married couples.

11. Always keep your words, and respect the rights of your spouse.

12. Choose a time - at least once a week - to spend together, doing something your partner enjoys.

13. Complete and discuss individual expectations exercises. Do not live with the assumption of what your spouse wants. Instead, tell each other what you expect of your spouse. Write your points down and discuss them. The more detailed you are, the more guesswork you take out of your expectations.

14. Your spouse can only trust you to the degree that he or she believes that you can resist the devil, resist the flesh, and make right choices on a consistent basis. Trust takes a lifetime to build, a second to destroy, and another lifetime to rebuild again!

15. Commit yourself, your spouse and your marriage to God, regularly. Be sensitive to the voice of the Spirit and be discerning enough to detect and reject the wiles of the evil one.

May God bless your home abundantly.

NOTES

NOTES

NOTES

NOTES